ACKNOWLEDGEMENTS

Thank you to my circle of friends and family who consistently give me the time, energy and inspiration to create and to fly.

Thank you to Harvard Law School. I complained passionately about your shortcomings respecting diversity, but the legacy of friendships and inspiring relationships that you gave me is incomparable, most notably President Barack Obama, but also so many others like Nicole, Rhonda, Stephanie R., Sully, Stephanie S., Ursula, Hill, Ken, David T., David H., David S., Brian, Spencer, Julie, Cassandra, Kim, Jodi, Sarah…and of course, Tree. You have all inspired me, made me laugh, made me cry, made me who I am today.

I owe a special thank you to Damien, who breathed life into this project when I thought there was nothing left.

And special thanks to my artist and friend, Ann Marie Williams, my mentor Dr. Shirley Malcom, my sister & brother-in-law Dawn & Corey, my cousin Candis, and to my mother.

Thank you to Mike & Lenny for your vision and passion for digibooks—the next generation of literacy.

And to my wonderful husband, Harvey and my children, I wouldn't be possible as I am without you.

Published by Brand Nu Words

1314 Fairmont Street NW
Washington, DC 20009
www.BrandNuWords.com

Brand Nu Words and the portrayal of the green digital book and mouse are trademarks of Brand Nu Words, LLC.

ISBN: 978-0-9748142-4-7
Library of Congress Control Number: 2008911406

First Edition: January 2009

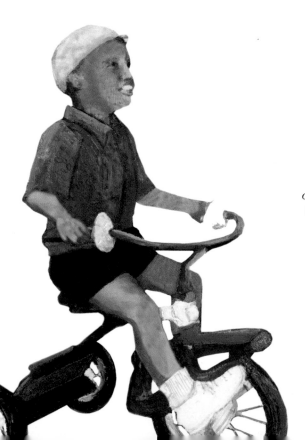

PREFACE

Author Charisse Carney-Nunes and Barack Obama as students at Harvard Law School in April 1991.

This book tells a story of how a child can change the world. It creates a space where children can experience the extraordinary life of President Barack Obama while imagining the possibilities for themselves. *I am Barack Obama* includes accounts of children already using this inspirational moment in history to imagine their futures in compelling ways, as captured by the powerful statement, "I am Barack Obama."

This author is proud and blessed to have called our new president a friend. I knew him long before he was president, as he attended Harvard Law School in the early 90s as a fellow student and participated in the school's Black Law Students Association (BLSA) that I presided over. I wish I could say I knew, at that point, this incredible man would one day be president of our nation. I can't. But many of us at Harvard did know this man was something very rare, and that something special was happening; for this was truly a man who wanted to change the world.

The success of President Obama is a lesson to be shared by all citizens—and especially all children—regardless of race, geography or income-level. It encourages us all to become agents of change in our own lives and in the lives of others; it encourages our children to grow into and become the very leaders they seek.

Since President Obama was elected, I have seen the impact on children. Their ears are attuned to his words. Their stride flows rhythmically with his step. I have seen them walk differently, talk differently, dress differently, and even think differently, all because of Barack. And while there is still much work to be done, I wanted to write this book because inspiration and optimism are the first steps. Children must believe before they can achieve. And President Obama's historic run is undeniable proof to our children that their lives are limited only by the possibilities they neglect to imagine.

—Charisse Carney-Nunes

Who will grab the sun and make it
shine through all our blues?

Who will chase the storm clouds
to the brightest rainbow's hue?

**Who will wrap the earth, my child,
in all that's good and true?**

Who will change the world,
my child?
It's you, oh yes, it's you!

It starts with just a simple dream
Born deep within my mind

That unity within our world
Should not be so hard to find.

I take my hopes and dreams for life
    And I Invest them all in you

I kiss your heart and mind
    And hope you'll have your own
    dreams too.

You will see the world, I know
  With hopefulness of youth

You will light our lives, my child
  With love and peace and truth.

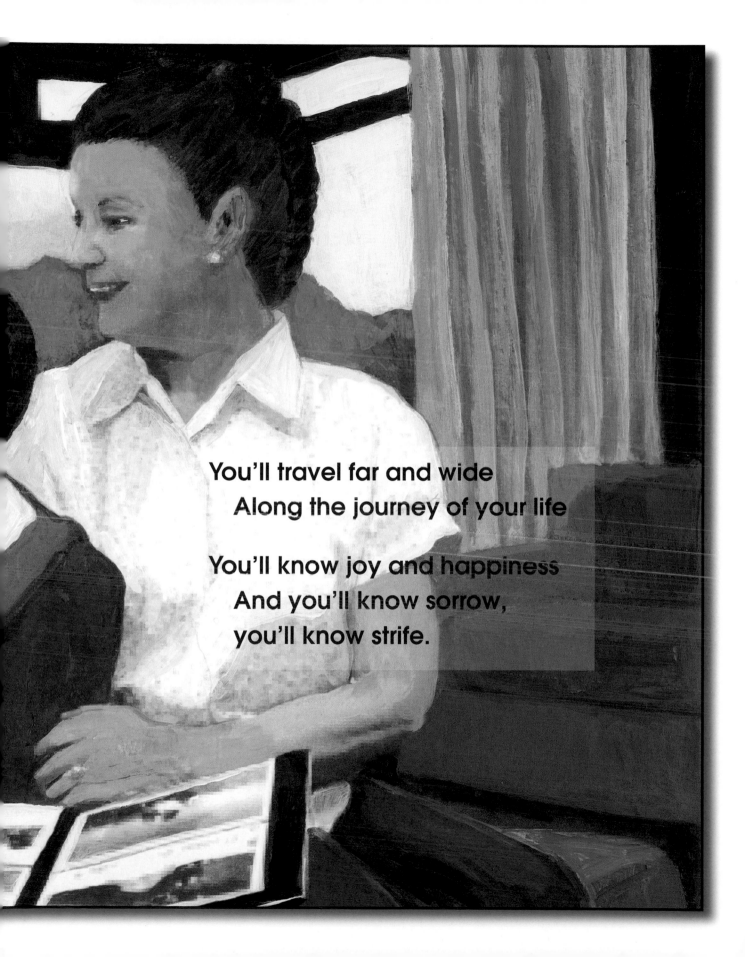

You'll travel far and wide
Along the journey of your life

You'll know joy and happiness
And you'll know sorrow,
you'll know strife.

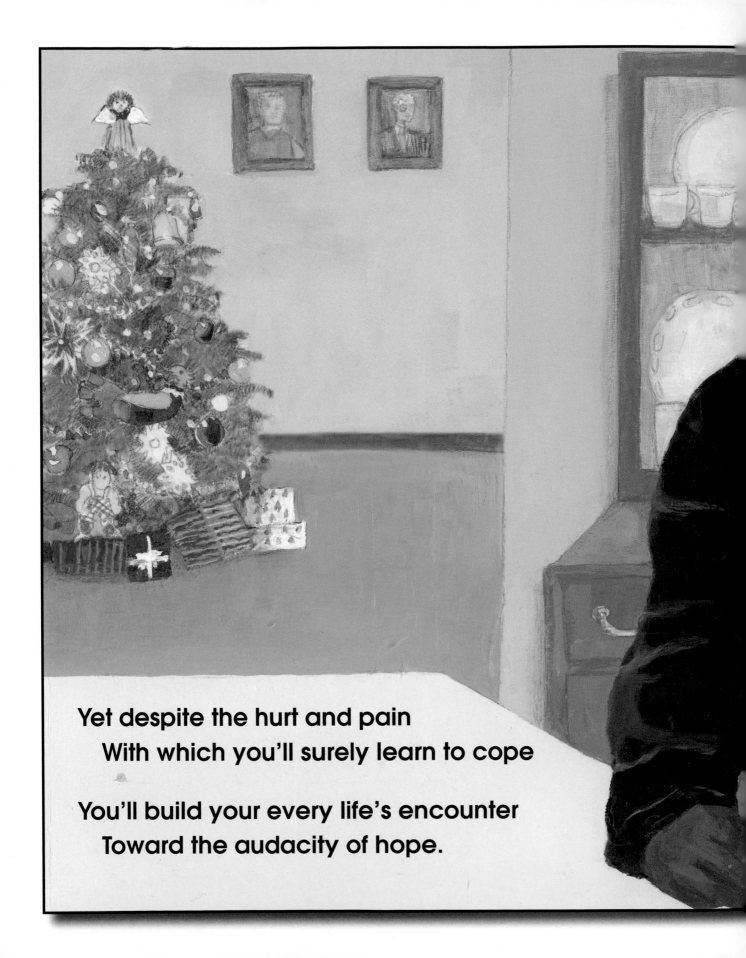

Yet despite the hurt and pain
   With which you'll surely learn to cope

You'll build your every life's encounter
   Toward the audacity of hope.

For all along the way
    You'll meet a thousand
    points of light

Lifting up your possibility
Imagining your heights.

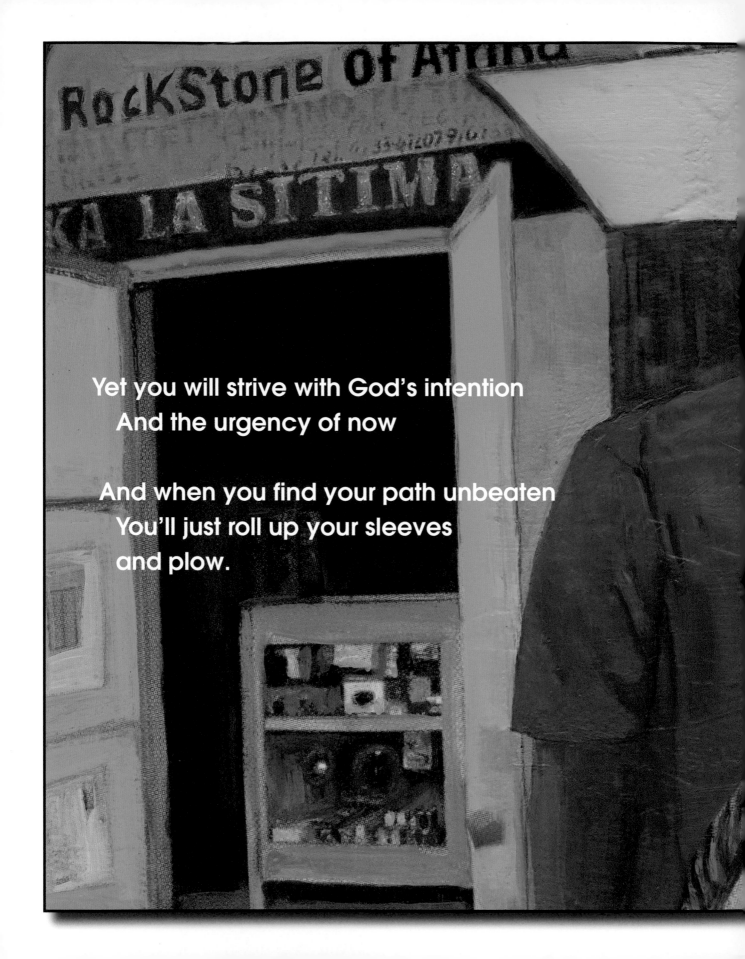

Yet you will strive with God's intention
    And the urgency of now

    And when you find your path unbeaten
    You'll just roll up your sleeves
    and plow.

And we all will be inspired
By the sheer distance
of your reach

And you will grab the sun and make
it shine through all our blues

And you will chase the storm clouds
to the brightest rainbow's hue.

BARACK'S STORY

PRESIDENT BARACK HUSSEIN OBAMA II was born in Hawaii in 1961. His father was a black African from Kenya and his mother was a white American. When he was two years old, Barack's parents divorced and his father returned to Kenya to continue his work in economics.

In 1967, Barack moved to Indonesia with his mom and her new husband. He eventually came back to Hawaii to live with his grandparents and finish high school. After high school, he left for Los Angeles to attend Occidental College and later transferred to Columbia University in New York. After graduating, Barack worked as a community organizer in the Chicago area before continuing his education at one of the best schools in the country, Harvard Law School. At Harvard, he became the first African-American president of one of the most important legal journals in the nation, the Harvard Law Review. After graduating as a top student and writing a book about his unique family, Barack worked as a law professor and a civil rights lawyer in the Chicago area.

While in Chicago, Barack taught classes at the University of Chicago's Law School. He also ran for public office and eventually became a State Senator for Illinois, a position where he could help people and make laws for his state.

In 2004, State Senator Obama started another political contest to become a United States Senator. During the contest, he made a major speech at the 2004 Democratic National Convention, an important event where the Democratic Party publicly supports its candidate for president. State Senator Obama's speech became known as one of the greatest speeches ever made. He went on to win his race and was elected as a U.S. Senator. At the time, he was the only African-American in the 100-member Senate.

On February 10, 2007, Senator Obama—knowing he could help people even more as president—announced that he was running for the top spot in the land. And on August 28, 2008 he became the first African-American to be nominated by either the Democrats or the Republicans as a candidate for the presidency of the United States.

On November 4, 2008 after an exciting and historic campaign, Barack Obama became the 44th President of the United States, and the first African American to ever win this position. President Obama is married to Michelle Robinson Obama, and they have two daughters, Malia Ann and Sasha.

SHARE YOUR STORY

Now that you have read Barack's story, go to **www.IAmBarackObamaBook.com** and let others know how he has inspired you.

Read the following pages to see what other children are saying.

"I am BARACK OBAMA"

LiMei
8 years old
Los Angeles, CA

Some people inspire one person, like my mama inspires me to be good. Some people inspire a whole movement, like Ruby Bridges who, when she was just a little girl like me, bravely went to a white school and now I can go to school with people of all races. Some people inspire the world, like Martin Luther King, Jr., who said what people didn't want to hear and ended up changing their minds.

America will improve because Barack Obama was elected as President. He will make good choices and treat everybody fairly. America is already changing because he is the first African-American president of the United States. African-Americans have been mistreated just because of the color of their skin. This is wrong. Before, Chinese people in America were mistreated too because of the color of our skin. There were laws that did not allow us to immigrate to the U.S., did not allow us to go to the same school as white children, and did not allow us to own our own homes. I am glad this has changed. African-American heroes who fought segregation also helped Chinese people.

There is still a lot of prejudice in this country, but Barack Obama believed in himself and believed in America. When my grandparents arrived, they were very poor and did not speak English, but they also believed in themselves and believed in America. President Obama shows that there are so many more possibilities now than in the past. He shows me that I can change the world by doing my best in everything I do and that even if we are different, we can all be anything we want to be. He has inspired the world, he inspired a movement, and he inspires me.

TREY
8 years old
Cambridge, MA

I know that just because we have an African-American president that everything will not be wonderful for people of color. Everyone and everything will not be perfectly fine when Mr. Obama steps into the oval office on January 20, 2009. But, we have seen a change you can believe in.

Just as in the movie The Great Debaters, we do what we have to do so we can do what we want to do. Obama studied hard, worked hard, helped others as a community organizer so he could be what he wanted to be, President of the United States.

Obama had a dream of becoming president and his dream came true. I know that anything that I dream of becoming be it an engineer, a famous author, a wealthy business man or even President of the United States can come true with hard work and determination. For now the dream of Dr. Martin Luther King Jr—"that my four children will one day live in a nation where they will not be judged by the color of their skin but by the content of their character," has become a reality.

My parents have always told me that each generation makes it better for the next generation. We, the future generation, must look at this enormous accomplishment and use it as an inspiration to push forward. As the Liberal Lion, Senator Edward M. Kennedy says, "the work begins anew; the hope rises again; and the dream lives on."

"I am BARACK OBAMA"

PEYTON
9 years old
Madison, WI

Barack Obama inspired me by setting the U.S. record, becoming the first person of color to be president. He acted like his motto was to do whatever you can to be what you want. No one and nothing can stop you.

When I saw him in a magazine with the other candidates, I knew right away I picked him. It struck me like thunder. He made a good effort, followed his dreams and won.

I went to see him speak in Madison, Wisconsin where I live. It was so amazing that he came all the way to Madison to talk to us even though there was a blizzard. That's a lot of dedication. There were so many people there that it took two hours for me to get to the door. After the speech, we were walking home. Barack's car went right past me. I took pictures. I was so excited I fell down in a huge snow bank behind me.

It is special that he is like me. I have some African heritage, too. But I have plenty of other heritages. His family is like my family. We are all related, but we have different personalities and heritages.

When I grow up I want to be an astronaut. Now Barack showed me that I can do it. Nobody can stop me from getting where I want to. Nothing will get in my way. Barack makes a lot of people know there are more things they can grow up to be.

SYDNEY & JILLIAN
8 years old
Princeton Junction, NJ

We have changed the world! We're only kids but Barack Obama has inspired us in many ways. He taught us not just to hope things will get better but actually go and make them better. He taught us not to care what people think about us but to care what we think about ourselves.

Barack Obama grew up in a very poor family during the times that black people weren't treated right but that didn't put him down, he pulled himself up. When he was running for president in the beginning and most people thought he was going to lose, that didn't get him down, it made him work harder. Even when people were mean to him, he wasn't mean back.

Our grandma told us that there was a lot prejudice against African-American people when she was a little girl like us. Our lives are different. We have lots of friends from different cultures and we are glad that we are able to go to the same school as them. Most of the people in our school voted for Barack Obama and they are mostly from different places. They are Chinese, Indian, White, Black and Latino but they are American and they believe in Barack Obama.

We wanted Barack Obama to be president so we campaigned for many days to make it happen. We discovered no matter how young we are, we are powerful enough to do anything. We can be nice to mean people. We can elect a president. We can change the world.

MORGANA
10 years old
Los Angeles, CA

The same year Barack Obama won, I won. I am currently the youngest president ever elected in my middle school. Everyone told me to run for secretary or treasurer—something "more realistic" they said. But in my reality, I am capable of being president of the middle school, so I didn't listen to them, and I ran for president.

Like Obama, my speech made all the difference. I was inspired by Obama's way of making people hopeful. He had such an easy way of presenting solutions, even I could understand him. So I made sure to present myself in a way that took my age and experience out of the question and focused on progress and hope. This connected with my classmates, and before I knew it I was voted the next president.

Obama has made history because he didn't see any barriers or limitations. He was just himself, just Obama. He showed us that barriers can be broken if you try. Never let anyone tell you something isn't possible. If they do, I have one word for you: "Obama!"

"I am BARACK OBAMA"

JACQUELINE
9 years old
Arlington, VA

Barack Obama is our new President; he is a very good man. I am so glad that he got elected because he is going to make this country a better place. I think Obama has some really good ideas. For example, he will give more money to educate kids under five, he will make math and science education a national priority, and he is going to put one million plug-in hybrid cars on the road by 2015.

My family and I worked so hard to help elect Obama to win—and he did! We canvassed door to door and we made posters to do visibility. We also helped organize a family fun day for Obama.

I am really excited because Obama is the first African-American President—ever! On Election Day, November 4th, my parents let me stay up a little later than usual, but not late enough to see who won the election. I couldn't sleep that night because I was afraid Obama would not win, but I still had hope. The first thing I did in the morning was rush down the stairs and look at the newspaper where I saw the words printed right on it "Obama Makes History!" When I saw that headline, I didn't even read the article. I just started dancing for joy!

I think Barack Obama is a great leader and I am excited about my future.

DYLAN
8 years old
Los Angeles, CA

When I was five years old I found a mouse pad with all the presidents on it. I noticed that there were only European Americans on it. So I went to my Mom and asked her, "Why are there only European Americans on this?" My Mom said because there has been a history of discrimination and only European Americans have had the opportunity to be President of the United States.

Since Barack Obama is the President I can say to myself, "I can be whatever I want." He gave me hope that the economy can be pulled back together and global warming will stop. I have put all my trust into him. He has the fate of our nation in his hands. Now the good thing is he seems like he is telling the truth.

The thing that I will do with my life differently is I will aim as high as possible in my job. I also want a good paying job so I can be happy and healthy. You may think this is too much away from the subject but really all of this is in his hands.

If Barack can help with the economy, I can have a good job that is productive and my job will not shut down. If Barack can lower health insurance bills I can go to the hospital and be able to pay the hospital. Nobody is perfectly healthy so you always need health insurance. I think Barack Obama is just what this country needs.

YUVENCA
10 years old
East Orange, NJ

Barack Obama inspires me in a lot of ways. I remember the day when he was elected as the next president of the United States. I was so excited that I cried. It was a marvelous moment in my life. Barack Obama inspires me to stay in school and to take my education seriously. He proved that being focused in school means you can become anything you want to be. And for Barack Obama, that means being the first African American to be elected as President of The United States of America.

Barack Obama also encourages me to never give up, believe in myself, and work my way to success. Back in the 1960's Dr. Martin Luther King Jr. said "I have seen the mountain top" and now, Barack Obama, our future president has reached the mountaintop.

When I see Barack Obama I see a ray of sunshine. I see a symbol of hope. Seeing Barack Obama makes me feel special and unique in my own way. I realize that a young girl like me can grow up and become President of the United States!

CLAIMING THE MOMENT
An Inaugural Tribute to Our Children

PRESIDENT BARACK OBAMA is a man of our times. Like King and Mandela before him, the emergence of this chosen bridge-builder is largely representative of the divisions that plague us, as well as our current demands for social progress. In other words, to employ a variation of a popular maxim, if Barack Obama weren't here, we'd have to invent him. Surely he has come along at the appropriate moment.

Like President Obama, this book, in both content and technology, strives to build bridges between communities regardless of race or space. The vivid illustrations of Ann Marie Williams portray Obama's multiracial family while depicting the varied geographic regions that nourished his childhood and influenced his later development. Rich scenes set in Hawaii, Indonesia, New York, Kenya, Boston and Chicago capture our president's internationalist perspective while supporting his unique position as an effective bridge-builder between different cultures and communities.

From a technological standpoint—one also consistent with Obama's internationalism—this book is offered in a leading-edge, interactive, digital format that allows it to be experienced online by communities across the globe. Children, libraries and schools from Kenya to Jakarta with online access will have the ability to virtually 'page through' this poetic expression and enjoy an experience similar to their U.S. counterparts. They will also have the ability to add digital content, sharing their stories about why our president inspires them to say, "I am Barack Obama."

This is only fitting, given that, for children, nothing is impossible. Their world is a pristine and magical place, less cluttered by the years of negative social conditioning that causes us by adulthood to dismiss any notions of human greatness or any developments that don't jive with our cynically constructed views of reality. Accordingly, when President Obama speaks of 'hope' and 'change,' children can automatically relate to such concepts without the pessimistic filter of maturity.

This is important since, ultimately, it is not up to us—those of us old enough to have marched with King or even those who organized for and witnessed the release and subsequent ascendancy of Mandela. Though we recognize that history is upon us, and the winds of change are brushing our awestruck faces, it is our children who will one day measure the true meaning of this moment. And while we acknowledge the immense nature of this development, history leaves it to their retrospective capacities to eventually determine just how big it actually is.

Even so, this moment is not about Barack Obama. I am sure our new president would agree that it is much bigger than him, notwithstanding his unprecedented electoral victory. For this moment belongs to the river of history as it winds along its sometimes turbulent path carrying its life-giving waters to our children, buoying their hopes and aspirations, creating new shoreline every step of the way. Rivers inherently transform the land mass around them, expanding paths and forging new openings over time. These openings are the domain of our children, theirs to explore, theirs to claim.

Similar to our 44th president and the generation of children he continues to impact, this book was borne of the river. It is my heartfelt contribution to the endless flow of history, to our timeless quest for human progress. And it is my childlike hope that—through these pages of poetic offering and upon these times of precedence and transformation—our current generation of children will sense that their moment is upon them, and that they, in fact, can change the world.

A CHILDREN'S CURRICULUM

AS PARENTS AND TEACHERS, it goes without saying that we have dreams for our children. That said, we ultimately want to instill in them the ability to dream and act for themselves. The work I do with The Jamestown Project is all about instilling these values in children. I am proud to describe the work of The Jamestown Project in this book because inspiring citizens—especially children—to become agents of change in their own lives exemplifies President Obama's message.

The Jamestown Project provides parents and teachers an effective tool for facilitating civic engagement among children. It is titled A Children's Curriculum for Civic Engagement, and it was released in the Fall of 2008 as part of the Children Do Democracy Too initiative, an outgrowth of our Doing Democracy work. The purpose of the initiative is to equip children with the knowledge and tools necessary to meaningfully participate in civil society and democracy. The central question we seek to answer is, "How do we instill the values of citizenship and active participation into the youngest, and in many ways the most important, members of our democracy?"

The curriculum is based on my second children's book, *I Dream For You a World: A Covenant For Our Children*. The Curriculum adapts concepts from the book into lessons and activities to promote civic engagement among elementary school children. The elementary grades are the age where children begin to understand their place in the world and their potential to make a difference in their own lives and the lives of their family, their community, and their country.

The Jamestown Project is currently piloting the curriculum and seeking new partners to help evaluate the program, share learning, and strategize on future goals. If you are interested in instilling the ideals of civic participation and optimism exemplified in President Obama's historic campaign, in children, then partner with us through your school, civic or educational program. Email us at info@jamestownproject.org.

www.jamestownproject.org